the elements of style

SIMPLIFIED & ILLUSTRATED FOR BUSY PEOPLE

William Strunk Jr.
Virginia Campbell

apostophes &
words ending in "s"

Form the possessive singular of nouns by adding 's'. Follow this rule whatever the final letter.

Thus write,

Charles's friend

Burns's poems

the witch's malice

commas in a list

In a series of three or more words with a single conjunction, use a comma after each word except the last.

Thus write,

red, white, and blue

gold, silver, or copper

He opened the letter, read it, and made a note of its contents.

In the names of business firms the last comma is omitted, as,

Brown, Shipley & Co.

commas for parentheticals

Enclose parenthetic phrases *between commas*.

> The best way to see a country, unless you are
> pressed for time, is to travel on foot.

This rule is difficult to apply; it is frequently hard to decide whether a single word, such as "however," or a brief phrase, is or is not parenthetic. If the interruption to the flow of the sentence is but *slight*, the writer may safely *omit* the commas. But whether the interruption be slight or considerable, he must never insert one comma and omit the other. Such punctuation as

> Marjorie's husband, Colonel Nelson paid us a visit
> yesterday,

or

> My brother you will be pleased to hear, is now in
> perfect health,

is indefensible.

commas for parentheticals (cont.)

If a parenthetic phrase is preceded by a conjunction (such as "and"), place the first comma *before* the conjunction, not after it.

> He saw us coming, and unaware that we had
> learned of his treachery, greeted us with a smile.

Always to be regarded as parenthetic and to be enclosed between commas (or, at the end of the sentence, between comma and period) are the following:

1. the year, when forming part of a date, and the day of the month, when following the day of the week:

> February to July, 1916.
> April 6, 1917.
> Monday, November 11, 1918.

2. the abbreviations "etc." and "jr."

commas for parentheticals

3. clauses which do not serve to identify or define the antecedent noun, and similar clauses introduced by conjunctions indicating time or place.

> The audience, which had at first been indifferent, became more and more interested.

In this sentence the clause introduced by "which" does not serve to tell which of several possible audiences is meant; what audience is in question is supposed to be already known. The clause adds, parenthetically, a statement supplementing that in the main clause. The sentence is virtually a combination of two statements which might have been made independently:

> The audience had at first been indifferent.
> It became more and more interested.

Compare the restrictive relative clause, not set off by commas, in the sentence,

> The candidate who best meets these requirements will obtain the place.

Here the clause introduced by "who" does serve to tell which of several possible candidates is meant; the sentence cannot be split up into two independent statements.

commas before conjunctions

Place a comma before a conjunction (such as "and") introducing a coordinate clause.

> The early records of the city have disappeared, and the story of its first years can no longer be reconstructed.

> The situation is perilous, but there is still one chance of escape.

Sentences of this type, isolated from their context, may seem to be in need of rewriting. As they make complete sense when the comma is reached, the second clause has the appearance of an afterthought.

Further, "and" is the least specific of connectives. Used between independent clauses, it indicates only that a relation exists between them without defining that relation. In the example above, the relation is that of cause and result. The two sentences might be rewritten:

> As the early records of the city have disappeared, the story of its first years can no longer be reconstructed.

> Although the situation is perilous, there is still one chance of escape.

commas cannot join clauses

If two or more clauses, grammatically complete and not joined by a conjunction (such as "and"), are to form *a single compound sentence*, the proper mark of punctuation is a *semicolon*.

> Stevenson's romances are entertaining; they are full of exciting adventures.
>
> It is nearly half past five; we cannot reach town before dark.

It is of course equally correct to write the above as two sentences each, replacing the semicolons by periods.

> Stevenson's romances are entertaining. They are full of exciting adventures.
>
> It is nearly half past five. We cannot reach town before dark.

If a conjunction is inserted the proper mark is a comma.

> Stevenson's romances are entertaining, for they are full of exciting adventures.
>
> It is nearly half past five, and we cannot reach town before dark.

commas cannot replace periods

Do not break sentences in two.
In other words, ***do not use periods for commas.***

> I met them on a Cunard liner several years ago.
> Coming home from Liverpool to New York.

> He was an interesting talker. A man who had
> traveled all over the world and lived in half a dozen
> countries.

In both these examples, the first period should be replaced
by a comma, and the following word begun with a small
letter.

It is permissible to make an emphatic word or expression serve the purpose of a sentence and to punctuate it
accordingly:

> Again and again he called out. No reply.

The writer must, however, be certain that the emphasis
is warranted, and that he will not be suspected of a mere
blunder in syntax or in punctuation.

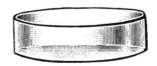

beware
dangling modifiers

A participial phrase at the beginning of a sentence must refer to the grammatical subject.

> Walking slowly down the road, he saw a woman accompanied by two children.

The word "walking" refers to the subject of the sentence, not to the woman. If the writer wishes to make it refer to the woman, he must recast the sentence:

> He saw a woman accompanied by two children, walking slowly down the road.

Participial phrases preceded by a conjunction or by a preposition, nouns in apposition, adjectives, and adjective phrases come under the same rule if they begin the sentence.

> **NO:** On arriving in Chicago, his friends met him at the station.
> **YES:** When he arrived in Chicago, his friends met him at the station.

Sentences violating this rule are often ludicrous.

> Being in a dilapidated condition, I was able to buy the house very cheap.

IV.
ELEMENTARY
PRINCIPLES
OF
COMPOSITION
(or: how to put the words together.)

one paragraph to each topic, please

If the subject on which you are writing is of slight extent, or if you intend to treat it very briefly, there may be no need of subdividing it into topics. Thus a brief description, a brief account of a single incident, a narrative merely outlining an action, the setting forth of a single idea, any one of these is best written in a single paragraph. After the paragraph has been written, examine it to see whether subdivision will not improve it.

Ordinarily, however, a subject requires subdivision into topics, each of which should be made the subject of a paragraph. The object of treating each topic in a paragraph by itself is, of course, to aid the reader. The beginning of each paragraph is a signal to him that a new step in the development of the subject has been reached.

In dialogue, each speech, even if only a single word, is a paragraph by itself; that is, a new paragraph begins with each change of speaker. The application of this rule, when dialogue and narrative are combined, is best learned from examples in well-printed works of fiction.

begin with a topic sentence

Again, the object is to **aid the reader.** The practice here recommended enables him to ***discover the purpose*** of each paragraph as he begins to read it, and to ***retain this purpose*** in mind as he ends it. For this reason, the most generally useful kind of paragraph, particularly in exposition and argument, is that in which

a. the topic sentence comes at or near the beginning;

b. the succeeding sentences explain or establish or develop the statement made in the topic sentence; and

c. the final sentence either emphasizes the thought of the topic sentence or states some important consequence.

Ending with a digression, or with an unimportant detail, is particularly **to be avoided.**

begin with a
topic sentence _(cont.)

If the paragraph forms part of a larger composition, its relation to what precedes, or its function as a part of the whole, may need to be expressed. This can sometimes be done by *a mere word or phrase* ("again"; "therefore"; "for the same reason") in the topic sentence.

Sometimes, however, it is expedient to precede the topic sentence by sentences of introduction or transition. If more than one such sentence is required, it is better to set apart the transitional sentences as a separate paragraph.

According to the writer's purpose, he may, as indicated above, relate the body of the paragraph to the topic sentence in one or more of several different ways.

He may make the meaning of the topic sentence clearer
by *restating it in other forms*,
by *defining its terms*,
by *denying the contrary*,
by *giving illustrations or specific instances*;
he may establish it *by proofs*;
or he may develop it *by showing its implications and consequences.*

In a long paragraph, he may carry out several of these processes.

20

begin with a
topic sentence (an example.)

1 Now, to be properly enjoyed, a walking tour should be gone upon alone. *2* If you go in a company, or even in pairs, it is no longer a walking tour in anything but name; it is something else and more in the nature of a picnic. *3* A walking tour should be gone upon alone, because freedom is of the essence; because you should be able to stop and go on, and follow this way or that, as the freak takes you; and because you must have your own pace, and neither trot alongside a champion walker, nor mince in time with a girl. *4* And you must be open to all impressions and let your thoughts take colour from what you see. *5* You should be as a pipe for any wind to play upon. *6* "I cannot see the wit," says Hazlitt, "of walking and talking at the same time. *7* When I am in the country, I wish to vegetate like the country," which is the gist of all that can be said upon the matter. *8* There should be no cackle of voices at your elbow, to jar on the meditative silence of the morning. *9* And so long as a man is reasoning he cannot surrender himself to that fine intoxication that comes of much motion in the open air, that begins in a sort of dazzle and sluggishness of the brain, and ends in a peace that passes comprehension.

--Stevenson, "Walking Tours"

use the
active voice

The active voice is usually more

direct & vigorous

than the passive.

> I shall always remember my first visit to Boston.

This is much better than:

> My first visit to Boston will always be remembered
> by me.

The first sentence is less direct, less bold, and less concise.
If the writer tries to make it more concise by omitting "by
me,"

> My first visit to Boston will always be remembered,

it becomes ***indefinite***: is it the writer, or some person un-
disclosed, or the world at large, that will always remember
this visit?

use the
active voice (cont.)

This rule does not, of course, mean that the writer should entirely discard the passive voice, which is frequently convenient and sometimes necessary.

> The dramatists of the Restoration are little esteemed today.

> Modern readers have little esteem for the dramatists of the Restoration.

The first would be the right form in a paragraph on the dramatists of the Restoration; the second, in a paragraph on the tastes of modern readers. The need of making a particular word the subject of the sentence will often, as in these examples, determine which voice is to be used.

A common fault is to use as the subject of a passive construction a noun which expresses the entire action, leaving the verb no function other than completing the sentence.

> NO: A survey of this region was made in 1900.
> YES: This region was surveyed in 1900.

> NO: Mobilization of the army was rapidly effected.
> YES: The army was rapidly mobilized.

use the
active voice (cont.)

The habitual use of the active voice makes for **_forcible writing_**. This is true not only in narrative principally concerned with action, but in writing of any kind.

Many a tame sentence of description or exposition can be made lively and emphatic by substituting a verb in the active voice for some such perfunctory expression as "there is," or "could be heard."

> NO: There were a great number of dead leaves
> lying on the ground.
> YES: Dead leaves covered the ground.
>
> NO: The sound of a guitar somewhere in the house
> could be heard.
> YES: Somewhere in the house a guitar hummed
> sleepily.
>
> NO: The reason that he left college was that his
> health became impaired.
> YES: Failing health compelled him to leave college.
>
> NO: It was not long before he was very sorry that he
> had said what he had.
> YES: He soon repented his words.

avoid the tame & non-committal

Put statements in positive form and make definite assertions. Avoid tame, colorless, hesitating, non-committal language. Use the word "not" as a means of denial or in antithesis, ***never as a means of evasion***.

> **NO:** He was not very often on time.
> **YES:** He usually came late.

> **NO:** He did not think that studying Latin was much use.
> **YES:** He thought the study of Latin useless.

> **NO:** "The Taming of the Shrew" is rather weak in spots. Shakespeare does not portray Katharine as a very admirable character, nor does Bianca remain long in memory as an important character in Shakespeare's works.
> **YES:** The women in "The Taming of the Shrew" are unattractive. Katharine is disagreeable, Bianca insignificant.

The last example, before correction, is indefinite as well as negative. The corrected version, consequently, is simply a guess at the writer's intention.

avoid the tame & non-committal

The word "not" is *inherently weak*. Consciously or unconsciously, the reader is dissatisfied with being told only what is not; he wishes to be told what is. Hence, as a rule, it is better to express even a negative in positive form.

not honest
dishonest

not important
trifling

did not remember
forgot

did not pay any attention to
ignored

did not have much confidence in
distrusted

The antithesis of negative and positive is strong:

Not charity, but simple justice.
Not that I loved Caesar less, but Rome the more.

Negative words other than "not" are usually strong:

The sun never sets upon the British flag.

specific, definite, & concrete

Prefer the specific to the general, the definite to the vague, the concrete to the abstract.

> **NO:** A period of unfavorable weather set in.
> **YES:** It rained every day for a week.
>
> **NO:** He showed satisfaction as he took possession of his well-earned reward.
> **YES:** He grinned as he pocketed the coin.

If those who have studied the art of writing are in accord on any one point, it is on this, that the surest method of arousing and holding the attention of the reader is by being *specific, definite, and concrete*.

The effectiveness of the greatest writers, Homer, Dante, Shakespeare, results from their constant

definiteness & concreteness.

Be specific.

Be definite.

Be concrete.

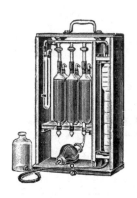

specific, definite, & concrete (cont.)

Prose, in particular narrative and descriptive prose, is made vivid by the same means.

If the experiences of Jim Hawkins and of David Balfour, of Kim, of Nostromo, have seemed for the moment *real* to countless readers, if in reading Carlyle we have almost *the sense of being physically present* at the taking of the Bastille, it is because of the definiteness of the details and the concreteness of the terms used.

It is not that *every* detail is given; that would be impossible, as well as to no purpose; but that all the *significant* details are given, and not vaguely, but with such definiteness that the reader, in imagination, can

project
himself
into the
scene.

specific, definite, & concrete (cont.)

In exposition and in argument, the writer must never lose his hold upon the concrete. Even when he is dealing with general principles, he must give particular instances of their application.

"This superiority of specific expressions is clearly due to the effort required to translate words into thoughts. As we do not think in generals, but in particulars--as whenever any class of things is referred to, we represent it to ourselves by calling to mind individual members of it, it follows that when an abstract word is used, the hearer or reader has to choose, from his stock of images, one or more by which he may figure to himself the genus mentioned. In doing this, some delay must arise, some force be expended; and if by employing a specific term an appropriate image can be at once suggested, an economy is achieved, and a more vivid impression produced."

Herbert Spencer, from whose "Philosophy of Style" the preceding paragraph is quoted, illustrates the principle:

> NO: In proportion as the manners, customs, and amusements of a nation are cruel and barbarous, the regulations of their penal code will be severe.

> YES: In proportion as men delight in battles, bull-fights, and combats of gladiators, will they punish by hanging, burning, and the rack.

omit
needless
words.

omit
needless words

Vigorous writing is concise. A sentence should contain **no unnecessary words**, a paragraph **no unnecessary sentences**, for the same reason that a drawing should have **no unnecessary lines** and a machine **no unnecessary parts**.

This requires not that the writer make all his sentences short, or that he avoid all detail and treat his subjects only in outline, but that he

make

every

word

tell.

delete
& write instead

(the question as to whether)
whether

(there is no doubt but that)
no doubt or doubtless

(used for fuel purposes)
used for fuel

(he is a man who)
he

(in a hasty manner)
hastily

(this is a subject which)
this subject

(His story is a strange one.)
His story is strange.

delete
"the fact that"

(owing to the fact that)
since or because

(in spite of the fact that)
though or although

(call your attention to the fact that)
remind you or notify you

(I was unaware of the fact that)
I was unaware that/I did not know that

(the fact that he had not succeeded)
his failure

(the fact that I had arrived)
my arrival

delete "who is" & "which was"

His brother, who is a member of the same firm
His brother, a member of the same firm

Trafalgar, which was Nelson's last battle
Trafalgar, Nelson's last battle

be concise

A positive statement is more concise than negative, and *the active voice* more concise than the passive.

A common violation of conciseness is the presentation of a single complex idea, step by step, in a series of sentences or independent clauses which might be combined into one.

> Macbeth was very ambitious. This led him to wish to become king of Scotland. The witches told him that this wish of his would come true. The king of Scotland at this time was Duncan. Encouraged by his wife, Macbeth murdered Duncan. He was thus enabled to succeed Duncan as king.
>
> (51 words.)
>
> Encouraged by his wife, Macbeth achieved his ambition and realized the prediction of the witches by murdering Duncan and becoming king of Scotland in his place.
>
> (26 words.)

avoid a string of loose sentences

An unskillful writer will sometimes construct a whole paragraph of sentences of this kind, using as connectives "and," "but," "so," and less frequently, "who," "which," "when," "where," and "while."

> The third concert of the subscription series was given last evening, and a large audience was in attendance. Mr. Edward Appleton was the soloist, and the Boston Symphony Orchestra furnished the instrumental music. The former showed himself to be an artist of the first rank, while the latter proved itself fully deserving of its high reputation. The interest aroused by the series has been very gratifying to the Committee, and it is planned to give a similar series annually.

Apart from its triteness and emptiness, the paragraph above is weak because of the structure of its sentences, with their ***mechanical symmetry and sing-song***.

If the writer finds that he has written a series of sentences of the type described, he should recast enough of them to remove the monotony, replacing them by simple sentences, by sentences of two clauses joined by a semicolon, by periodic sentences of two clauses, by sentences, loose or periodic, of three clauses--whichever best represent the real relations of the thought.

master parallel construction

Parallel construction requires that expressions of similar content and function should be outwardly similar. *The likeness of form* enables the reader to recognize more readily *the likeness of content and function*.

The unskillful writer often violates this principle, from a mistaken belief that he should constantly vary the form of his expressions. It is true that in repeating a statement in order to emphasize it he may have need to vary its form. But apart from this, he should follow the principle of parallel construction.

> NO: Formerly, science was taught by the textbook method, while now the laboratory method is employed.

> YES: Formerly, science was taught by the textbook method; now it is taught by the laboratory method.

The first version gives the impression that the writer is *undecided or timid*; he seems unable or afraid to choose one form of expression and hold to it. The second version shows that the writer has at least made his choice and abided by it.

master parallel construction (cont.)

By this principle, an article or a preposition applying to all the members of a series must either be used only before the first term or else be repeated before each term.

> **NO:** The French, the Italians, Spanish, and Portuguese
> **YES:** The French, the Italians, the Spanish, and the Portuguese
>
> **NO:** In spring, summer, or in winter
> **YES:** In spring, summer, or winter
> **OR:** In spring, in summer, or in winter

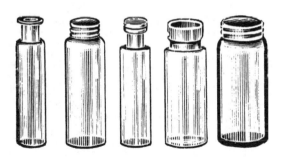

master parallel
construction (cont.)

Correlative expressions ("both, and;" "not, but;" "not only, but also;""either, or;" "first, second, third;" and the like) should be followed by the same grammatical construction, that is, virtually, by the same part of speech.

Many violations of this rule (as the first three below) arise from faulty arrangement; others (as the last) from the use of unlike constructions.

> **NO:** It was both a long ceremony and very tedious.
> **YES:** The ceremony was both long and tedious.
>
> **NO:** A time not for words, but action.
> **YES:** A time not for words, but for action.
>
> **NO:** Either you must grant his request or incur his ill will.
> **YES:** You must either grant his request or incur his ill will.
>
> **NO:** My objections are, first, the injustice of the measure; second, that it is unconstitutional.
> **YES:** My objections are, first, that the measure is unjust; second, that it is unconstitutional.

keep related words together

The position of the words in a sentence is the principal means of showing their relationship. The writer must therefore, so far as possible, *bring together the words*, and groups of words, *that are related in thought*, and keep apart those which are not so related. The subject of a sentence and the principal verb should not, as a rule, be separated by a phrase or clause that can be transferred to the beginning.

> **NO:** Wordsworth, in the fifth book of "The Excursion," gives a minute description of this church.
>
> **YES:** In the fifth book of "The Excursion," Wordsworth gives a minute description of this church.

> **NO:** Cast iron, when treated in a Bessemer converter, is changed into steel.
>
> **YES:** By treatment in a Bessemer converter, cast iron is changed into steel.

The objection is that the interposed phrase or clause needlessly *interrupts the natural order of the main clause*. Usually, however, this objection does not hold when the order is interrupted only by a relative clause or by an expression in apposition. Nor does it hold in periodic sentences in which the interruption is a deliberately used means of creating suspense.

keep related words together _(cont.)

The relative pronoun should come, as a rule, immediately after its antecedent.

> NO: He wrote three articles about his adventures in Spain, which were published in "Harper's Magazine."
> YES: He published in "Harper's Magazine" three articles about his adventures in Spain.

> NO: This is a portrait of Benjamin Harrison, grandson of William Henry Harrison, who became President in 1889.
> YES: This is a portrait of Benjamin Harrison, grandson of William Henry Harrison. He became President in 1889.

If the antecedent consists of a group of words, the relative comes at the end of the group, unless this would cause ambiguity.

> NO: A proposal to amend the Sherman Act, which has been variously judged.
> YES: A proposal, which has been variously judged, to amend the Sherman Act.
> OR: A proposal to amend the much-debated Sherman Act.

> NO: The grandson of William Henry Harrison, who
> YES: William Henry Harrison's grandson, who

keep related
words together _(cont.)

A noun in apposition may come between antecedent and relative, because in such a combination no real ambiguity can arise.

> The Duke of York, his brother, who was regarded with hostility by the Whigs

Modifiers should come, if possible, next to the word they modify. If several expressions modify the same word, they should be so arranged that no wrong relation is suggested.

> **NO:** All the members were not present.
> **YES:** Not all the members were present.

> **NO:** He only found two mistakes.
> **YES:** He found only two mistakes.

> **NO:** Major R. E. Joyce will give a lecture on Tuesday evening in Bailey Hall, to which the public is invited, on "My Experiences in Mesopotamia" at eight P. M.
> **YES:** On Tuesday evening at eight P. M., Major R. E. Joyce will give in Bailey Hall a lecture on "My Experiences in Mesopotamia." The public is invited.

keep to one tense

Whichever tense the writer chooses, he should use throughout. *Shifting from one tense to the other gives the appearance of uncertainty and irresolution.*

In presenting the statements or the thought of some one else, as in summarizing an essay or reporting a speech, the writer should avoid intercalating such expressions as "he said," "he stated," "the speaker added," "the speaker then went on to say," "the author also thinks," or the like.

He should indicate clearly at the outset, once for all, that what follows is summary, and then waste no words in repeating the notification.

But in the criticism or interpretation of literature the writer should be careful to avoid dropping into summary. He may find it necessary to devote one or two sentences to indicating the subject, or the opening situation, of the work he is discussing; he may cite numerous details to illustrate its qualities. But he should aim to *write an orderly discussion supported by evidence, not a summary with occasional comment.*

Similarly, if the scope of his discussion includes a number of works, he will as a rule do better not to take them up singly in chronological order, but to aim from the beginning at establishing general conclusions.

IV.
A FEW
MATTERS
OF FORM
(or: 5 easy ways to impress)

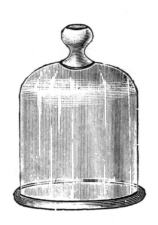

HEADINGS

Leave a blank line, or its equivalent in space, after the title or heading of a manuscript. On succeeding pages begin on the first line.

NUMERALS

Do not spell out dates or other numbers. Write them in figures or in Roman numerals, as may be appropriate.

> August 9, 1918 (9 August 1918)
> Rule 3
> Chapter XII
> 352nd Infantry

PARENTHESES

A sentence containing an expression in parenthesis is punctuated, outside of the marks of parenthesis, exactly as if the expression in parenthesis were absent. The expression within is punctuated as if it stood by itself, except that the final period is omitted *unless it is a question mark or an exclamation point.*

> I went to his house yesterday (my third attempt to see him), but he had left town.
>
> He declares (and why should we doubt his good faith?) that he is now certain of success.

(When a wholly detached sentence is parenthesized, the final punctuation comes before the last parenthesis.)

QUOTATIONS

Formal quotations, cited as evidence, are introduced by a colon and enclosed in quotation marks.

> The provision of the Constitution is: "No tax or duty shall be laid on articles exported from any state."

Quotations that are the direct objects of verbs are preceded by a comma and enclosed in quotation marks.

> I recall the maxim of La Rochefoucauld, "Gratitude is a lively sense of benefits to come."

> Aristotle says, "Art is an imitation of nature."

Quotations introduced by "that" are regarded as in indirect discourse and not enclosed in quotation marks.

> Keats declares that beauty is truth, truth beauty.

Proverbial expressions and familiar phrases of literary origin require no quotation marks.

> These are the times that try men's souls.
> He lives far from the madding crowd.

The same is true of colloquialisms and slang.

TITLES

For the titles of literary works, scholarly usage prefers italics with capitalized initials. The usage of editors and publishers varies, some using italics with capitalized initials, others using Roman with capitalized initials and with or without quotation marks.

Use italics, except in writing for a periodical that follows a different practice.

V.

WORDS
& EXPRESSIONS
COMMONLY
MISUSED
(or: don't make these errors.)

but first, a note

Some of the forms here listed, as "like I did," are **downright bad English**; others, as the split infinitive, have their defenders, but are in such general disfavor that it is at least inadvisable to use them; still others, as "case", "factor," "feature," "interesting," "one of the most," are good in their place, but are constantly obtruding themselves into places where they have no right to be.

If the writer will make it his purpose from the beginning to express accurately his own individual thought, and will **refuse to be satisfied with a ready-made formula** that saves him the trouble of doing so, this last set of expressions will cause him little trouble.

But if he finds that in a moment of inadvertence he has used one of them, his proper course will probably be not to patch up the sentence by substituting one word or set of words for another, but to **recast it completely**, as illustrated in a number of examples below.

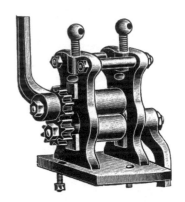

All right.
Idiomatic in familiar speech as a detached phrase in the sense, "Agreed," or "Go ahead." In other uses better avoided. Always written as two words.

As good or better than.
Expressions of this type should be corrected by rearranging the sentence.

> **NO:** My opinion is as good or better than his.
> **YES:** My opinion is as good as his, or better (if not better).

As to whether.
"Whether" is sufficient.

Bid.
Takes the infinitive without "to."
The past tense in the sense, "ordered," is "bade."

But.
Unnecessary after "doubt" and "help."

> NO: I have no doubt but that
> YES: I have no doubt that

> NO: He could not help see but that
> YES: He could not help seeing that

The too frequent use of "but" as a conjunction leads to *loose sentences*. A loose sentence formed with "but" can always be converted into a periodic sentence formed with "although."

Particularly awkward is the following of one "but" by another, making a contrast to a contrast or a reservation to a reservation. This is easily corrected by re-arrangement.

> NO: America had vast resources, but she seemed
> almost wholly unprepared for war. But within a
> year she had created an army of four million
> men.

> YES: America seemed almost wholly unprepared
> for war, but she had vast resources. Within
> a year she had created an army of four million
> men.

Can.
Means "am (is, are) able."
Not to be used as a substitute for "may."

Case.
The Concise Oxford Dictionary begins its definition of this word: "instance of a thing's occurring; usual state of affairs." In these two senses, the word is usually unnecessary.

> **NO:** In many cases, the rooms were poorly ventilated.
> **YES:** Many of the rooms were poorly ventilated.

> **NO:** It has rarely been the case that any mistake has been made.
> **YES:** Few mistakes have been made.

Certainly.
Used indiscriminately by some writers, much as others use "very" to intensify any and every statement.

A mannerism of this kind,
bad in speech,
is even worse in writing.

Character.
Often simply redundant, used from a mere habit of

wordiness.

> **NO:** Acts of a hostile character
> **YES:** Hostile acts

Claim, vb.
With object-noun, means "lay claim to." May be used with a dependent clause if this sense is clearly involved:

> He claimed that he was the sole surviving heir.

(But even here, "claimed to be" would be better.) Not a substitute for "declare," "maintain," or "charge."

Clever.
This word has been greatly overused; it is best restricted to **ingenuity displayed in small matters**.

Compare.
To "compare to" is to point out or imply resemblances, between objects regarded as essentially of different order; to "compare with" is mainly to point out differences, between objects regarded as essentially of the same order.

Thus life has been compared to a pilgrimage, to a drama, to a battle; Congress may be compared with the British Parliament. Paris has been compared to ancient Athens; it may be compared with modern London.

Consider.

Not followed by "as" when it means "believe to be."

> I consider him thoroughly competent.

Compare, "The lecturer considered Cromwell first as soldier and second as administrator," where "considered" means "examined" or "discussed."

Data.

A plural, like "phenomena" and "strata."

> These data were tabulated.

Dependable.

A needless substitute for "reliable," "trustworthy."

Different than.

Not permissible. Substitute "different from," "other than," or "unlike."

Divided into.

Not to be misused for "composed of."
The line is sometimes difficult to draw; doubtless plays are divided into acts, but poems are composed of stanzas.

Don't.

Contraction of "do not."

The contraction of "does not" is "doesn't."

Due to.

Incorrectly used for "through," "because of," or "owing to," in adverbial phrases:

> He lost the first game, due to carelessness.

In correct use related as predicate or as modifier to a particular noun:

> This invention is due to Edison
>
> Losses due to preventable fires

Folk.

A collective noun, equivalent to "people." Use the singular form only.

Effect.

As noun, means "result;" as verb, means "to bring about," "accomplish" (not to be confused with "affect," which means "to influence"). As noun, often loosely used in perfunctory writing about fashions, music, painting, and other arts: "an Oriental effect;" "effects in pale green;" "a charming effect was produced by."

The writer who has a definite meaning to express will not take refuge in *such vagueness.*

Etc.

Equivalent to "and the rest," "and so forth," and hence not to be used if one of these would be insufficient, that is, if the reader would be left in doubt as to any important particulars. Least open to objection when it represents the last terms of a list already given in full, or immaterial words at the end of a quotation.

At the end of a list introduced by "such as," "for example," or any similar expression, "etc." is incorrect.

Fact.

Use this word only of matters of a kind capable of direct verification, not of matters of judgment. That a particular event happened on a given date, that lead melts at a certain temperature, are facts. But such conclusions as that Napoleon was the greatest of modern generals, or that the climate of California is delightful, however incontestable

they may be, are not properly facts.

Factor.

A hackneyed word; the expressions of which it forms part can usually be replaced by something more direct and idiomatic.

> NO: His superior training was the great factor in his winning the match.
> YES: He won the match by being better trained.

Feature.

Another hackneyed word; like "factor" it usually adds nothing to the sentence in which it occurs.

> A feature of the entertainment especially worthy of mention was the singing of Miss A.

(Better use the same number of words to tell what Miss A. sang, or if the program has already been given, to tell how she sang.)

As a verb, in the advertising sense of "offer as a special attraction," to be avoided.

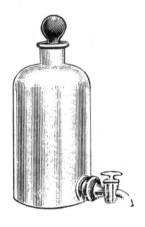

Get.

The colloquial "have got" for "have" should not be used in writing. The preferable form of the participle is "got."

He is a man who.

A common type of redundant expression.

NO: He is a man who is very ambitious.
YES: He is very ambitious.

Help.

See under "But."

However.

In the meaning "nevertheless," not to come first in it sentence or clause.

> **NO:** The roads were almost impassable. However, we at last succeeded in reaching camp.
>
> **YES:** The roads were almost impassable. At last, however, we succeeded in reaching camp.

When "however" comes first, it means "in whatever way" or "to whatever extent."

> **NO:** However you advise him, he will probably do as he thinks best.
>
> **YES:** However discouraging the prospect, he never lost heart.

Interesting.

Avoid this word as a perfunctory means of introduction.

Instead of announcing that what you are about to tell is interesting,

make it SO.

"An interesting story is told of..."
(Tell the story without preamble.)

Kind of/sort of

Not to be used as a substitute for "rather" (before adjectives and verbs), or except in familiar style, for "something like" (before nouns). Restrict it to its literal sense:

> Amber is a kind of fossil resin.
> I dislike that sort of notoriety.

Less.

Should not be misused for "fewer."

> **NO:** He had less men than in the previous campaign.
> **YES:** He had fewer men than in the previous campaign.

"Less" refers to quantity, "fewer" to number. "His troubles are less than mine" means "His troubles are not so great as mine." "His troubles are fewer than mine" means "His troubles are not so numerous as mine."

It is, however, correct to say, "The signers of the petition were less than a hundred," where the round number "a hundred" is something like a collective noun, and "less" is thought of as meaning a less quantity or amount.

Like.

Not to be misused for "as." "Like" governs nouns and pronouns; before phrases the equivalent word is "as."

> **NO:** We spent the evening like in the old days.
> **YES:** We spent the evening as in the old days.

Line, along these lines.

"Line" in the sense of "course of procedure," "conduct," "thought," is allowable, but has been so much over-worked, particularly in the phrase "along these lines," that a writer who aims at freshness or originality had better discard it entirely.

> **NO:** Mr. B. also spoke along the same lines.
> **YES:** Mr. B. also spoke, to the same effect.

> **NO:** He is studying along the line of French literature.
> **YES:** He is studying French literature.

Literal, literally.

Often incorrectly used in support of exaggeration or violent metaphor.

> **NO:** A literal flood of abuse.
> **YES:** A flood of abuse.

> **NO:** Literally dead with fatigue
> **YES:** Almost dead with fatigue (dead tired)

Lose out.

Meant to be more emphatic than "lose," but actually less so, because of its commonness. The same holds true of "try out," win out,""sign up," "register up."

With a number of verbs, "out" and "up" form idiomatic combinations: "find out," "run out," "turn out," "cheer up," "dry up," "make up," and others, each distinguishable in meaning from the simple verb. "Lose out" is not.

Most.

Not to be used for "almost."

> NO: Most everybody
> YES: Almost everybody
>
> NO: Most all the time
> YES: Almost all the time

Nature.

Often simply redundant, used like "character."

> NO: Acts of a hostile nature
> YES: Hostile acts

Often vaguely used in such expressions as a "lover of nature;" "poems about nature."

Unless more specific statements follow, the reader cannot tell whether the poems have to do with natural scenery, rural life, the sunset, the untracked wilderness, or the habits of squirrels.

Near by.

Adverbial phrase, not yet fully accepted as good English, though the analogy of "close by" and "hard by" seems to justify it.

"Near," or "near at hand," is as good, if not better. Not to be used as an adjective; use "neighboring."

Oftentimes, ofttimes.

Archaic forms, no longer in good use. The modern word is "often."

One hundred and one.

Retain the "and" in this and similar expressions, in accordance with the unvarying usage of English prose from Old English times.

One of the most.

Avoid beginning essays or paragraphs with this formula, as, "One of the most interesting developments of modern science is, etc.;" "Switzerland is one of the most interesting countries of Europe."

There is nothing wrong in this; it is simply

threadbare and forcible-feeble.

A common blunder is to use a singular verb in a relative clause following this or a similar expression, when the relative is the subject.

> NO: One of the ablest men that has attacked this problem.
> YES: One of the ablest men that have attacked this problem.

Participle for verbal noun.

NO: Do you mind me asking a question?
YES: Do you mind my asking a question?

NO: There was little prospect of the Senate
accepting even this compromise.
YES: There was little prospect of the Senate's
accepting even this compromise.

The construction shown in the second example is occasionally found and has its defenders. Yet it is easy to see that the second sentence has to do not with a prospect of the Senate, but with a prospect of accepting. In this example, at least, the construction is plainly illogical.

People.

"The people" is a political term, not to be confused with "the public." From the people comes political support or opposition; from the public comes artistic appreciation or commercial patronage.

Phase.

Means a stage of transition or development: "the phases of the moon;" "the last phase." Not to be used for "aspect" or "topic."

NO: Another phase of the subject
YES: Another point

Possess.

Not to be used as a mere substitute for "have" or "own."

> NO: He possessed great courage.
> YES: He had great courage (was very brave).

> NO: He was the fortunate possessor of
> YES: He owned

Prove.

The past participle is "proved."

Respective, respectively.

These words may usually be omitted with advantage.

> NO: Works of fiction are listed under the names
> of their respective authors.
> YES: Works of fiction are listed under the names
> of their authors.

> NO: The one mile and two mile runs were won
> by Jones and Cummings respectively.
> YES: The one mile and two mile runs were won
> by Jones and by Cummings.

In some kinds of formal writing, as geometrical proofs, it may be necessary to use "respectively," but it should not appear in writing on ordinary subjects.

Shall, Will.

The future tense requires "shall" for the first person, "will" for the second and third. The formula to express the speaker's belief regarding his future action or state is "I shall;" "I will" expresses his determination or his consent.

Should.

See under "Would."

So.

Avoid, in writing, the use of "so" as an intensifier: "so good;" "so warm;" "so delightful."

Sort of.

See under "Kind of."

Split Infinitive.

There is precedent from the fourteenth century downward for interposing an adverb between "to" and the infinitive which it governs, but the construction is in disfavor and is avoided by nearly all careful writers.

> **NO:** To diligently inquire
> **YES:** To inquire diligently

State.

Not to be used as a mere substitute for "say", "remark." Restrict it to the sense of "express fully or clearly," as, "He refused to state his objections."

Student Body.

A needless and awkward expression meaning no more than the simple word "students."

> **NO:** A member of the student body
> **YES:** A student

> **NO:** The student body passed resolutions.
> **YES:** The students passed resolutions.

System.

Frequently used without need.

> **NO:** Dayton has adopted the commission system of government.
> **YES:** Dayton has adopted government by commission.

> **NO:** The dormitory system
> **YES:** Dormitories

Thanking You in Advance.

This sounds as if the writer meant, "It will not be worth my while to write to you again."

In making your request, write, "Will you please," or "I shall be obliged," and if anything further seems necessary write a letter of acknowledgment later.

They.

A common inaccuracy is the use of the plural pronoun when the antecedent is a distributive expression such as "each," "each one," "everybody," "every one," "many a man," which, though implying more than one person, requires the pronoun to be in the singular.

Similar to this, but with even less justification, is the use of the plural pronoun with the antecedent "anybody," "any one," "somebody," "some one," the intention being either to avoid the awkward "he or she," or to avoid committing oneself to either. Some bashful speakers even say, "A friend of mine told me that they, etc."

Use "he" with all the above words, unless the antecedent is or must be feminine.

Very.

Use this word sparingly. Where emphasis is necessary, use words strong in themselves.

Viewpoint.

Write "point of view," but do not misuse this, as many do, for "view" or "opinion."

While.

Avoid the indiscriminate use of this word for "and," but," and "although."

Many writers use it as a substitute for "and" or "but," either from a mere desire to vary the connective, or from uncertainty which of the two connectives is the more appropriate. In this use it is best replaced by a semicolon.

> **NO:** The office and salesrooms are on the ground floor, while the rest of the building is devoted to manufacturing.
> **YES:** The office and salesrooms are on the ground floor; the rest of the building is devoted to manufacturing.

Compare:

> **NO:** While the temperature reaches 90 or 95 degrees in the daytime, the nights are often chilly.
> **YES:** Although the temperature reaches 90 or 95 degrees in the daytime, the nights are often chilly.

The paraphrase,
"The temperature reaches 90 or 95 degrees in the daytime; at the same ime the nights are often chilly,"
shows why the use of "while" is incorrect.

In general, the writer will do well to use "while" only with strict literalness, in the sense of "during the time that."

Whom.

Often incorrectly used for "who" before "he said" or similar expressions, when it is really the subject of a following verb.

NO: His brother, whom he said would send him
the money
YES: His brother, who he said would send him
the money

NO: The man whom he thought was his friend
YES: The man who (that) he thought was his friend
(whom he thought his friend)

Worth while.

Overworked as a term of vague approval and (with "not") of disapproval. Strictly applicable only to actions: "Is it worth while to telegraph?"

NO: His books are not worth while.
YES: His books are not worth reading (are not worth
one's while to read; do not repay reading;
are worthless).

The use of "worth while" before a noun ("a worth while story") is indefensible.

Would.

A conditional statement in the first person requires "should," not "would."

> I should not have succeeded without his help.

The equivalent of "shall" in indirect quotation after a verb in the past tense is "should," not "would."

> He predicted that before long we should have a great surprise.

To express habitual or repeated action, the past tense, without "would," is usually sufficient, and from its brevity, more emphatic.

> **NO:** Once a year he would visit the old mansion.
> **YES:** Once a year he visited the old mansion.

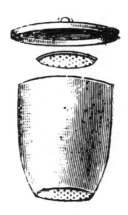

VI.

SPELLING

(or: words to watch out for.)

The spelling of English words is not fixed
and invariable, nor does it depend on any other authority
than general agreement. At the present day there is prac-
tically unanimous agreement as to the spelling of most
words.

In the list below, for example, "rime" for "rhyme" is the
only allowable variation; all the other forms are co-ex-
tensive with the English language. At any given moment,
however, a relatively small number of words may be
spelled in more than one way.

Gradually, as a rule, one of these forms comes to be
generally preferred, and the less customary form comes
to look obsolete and is discarded. From time to time new
forms, mostly simplifications, are introduced by innova-
tors, and either win their place or die of neglect.

Why does spelling matter?

The practical objection to unaccepted and over-simplified
spellings is the disfavor with which they are received by
the reader. They distract his attention and exhaust his
patience.

He reads the form "though" automatically, without
thought of its needless complexity; he reads the
abbreviation "tho" and mentally supplies the missing
letters, at the cost of a fraction of his attention. The writer
has defeated his own purpose.

words often misspelled

accidental
advice
affect
believe
benefit
challenge
coarse
course
criticize
deceive
definite
describe
despise
develop
disappoint
dissipate
duel

ecstasy
effect
embarrass
existence
fascinate
fiery
formerly
humorous
hypocrisy
immediately
impostor
incident
incidentally
latter
led
lose
marriage
mischief
murmur
necessary
occurred
opportunity
parallel
Philip
playwright
preceding
prejudice
principal
principle
privilege
pursue

repetition
rhyme
rhythm
ridiculous
sacrilegious
seize
separate
shepherd
siege
similar
simile
too
tragedy
tries
undoubtedly
until
villain

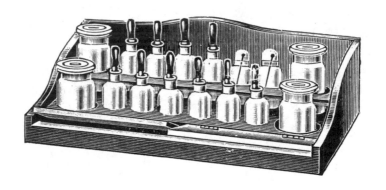

Was this the cure you needed?

Did you find this book helpful?

If so, would you consider paying it forward
by leaving a review on Amazon? It'll save
the next person the embarrassment
of weak writing and sloppy spelling!

about the author

William Strunk, Jr. was a professor of English at Cornell University. In 1918, he self-published *The Elements of Style* for his students, which quickly became known simply as "the little book."

This little book of rules for persuasive and powerful writing is as essential today as it was a hundred years ago, and *The Elements of Style* continues to live on in the millions of readers who have become better writers after spending some time with Professor Strunk.

about the editor

Virginia Campbell has worked as a writer, editor, and publisher for two decades. She's helped hundreds of writers Strunk-ify their writing and publish bestselling and award-winning books.

She lives in Georgia with her husband, daughter, and an illiterate Scottish Terrier. Her life goal is to work up enough courage to have "specific, definite, concrete" tattooed on her arm.

Ten percent of proceeds from the sale of this book
will be donated to the Free Minds Book Club,
which provides books and creative writing workshops
to incarcerated adults.

Thank you for supporting our mission
through the purchase of this book.

CPSIA information can be obtained
at www.ICGtesting.com
Printed in the USA
LVHW082352240519
619116LV00007B/16/P